IMAN VELLANI

BY JOANNE MATTERN

AMICUS LEARNING

Inspire is published by
Amicus Learning, an imprint of Amicus
P.O. Box 227
Mankato, MN 56002
www.amicuspublishing.us

Editor: Ana Brauer
Series Designer: Kathleen Petelinsek
Book Designer and Photo Researcher: Emily Dietz

Library of Congress Cataloging-in-Publication Data
Names: Mattern, Joanne, 1963- author
Title: Iman Vellani / Joanne Mattern.
Description: Mankato, MN : Amicus Learning, 2026. | Series: Inspire | Includes bibliographical references and index. | Audience: Ages 5-9 | Audience: Grades 2-3 | Summary: "From Marvel superfan to superhero! This engaging biography explores how Iman Vellani went from an ordinary teenager to playing Kamala Khan in *Ms. Marvel* and writing comics. Includes table of contents, glossary, further resources, and index"— Provided by publisher.
Identifiers: LCCN 2025011932 (print) | LCCN 2025011933 (ebook) | ISBN 9798892008600 library binding | ISBN 9798892009263 paperback | ISBN 9798892009928 ebook
Subjects: LCSH: Vellani, Iman | Motion picture actors and actresses—Canada—Biography—Juvenile literature | LCGFT: Biographies
Classification: LCC PN2308.V45 M38 2026 (print) | LCC PN2308.V45 (ebook) | DDC 791.4302/8092 [B]—dc23/eng/20250325
LC record available at https://lccn.loc.gov/2025011932
LC ebook record available at https://lccn.loc.gov/2025011933

Photo Credits: Alamy Stock Photo/AJ Pics, 7, Album, 14, Collection Christophel, 13, TCD/Prod.DB, 5; Associated Press/Chris Pizzello, cover; Getty Images/Mark Von Holden/Variety, 17, Mike Coppola, 21, Richard Lautens, 18, Tristan Fewings, 10-11, VALERIE MACON, 9; Shutterstock/Hseena, 8, Q world, 6

Printed in the United States of America

Table of Contents

Many Talents

Iman Vellani is a young actress. She played Kamala Khan in a TV show and a movie. Khan is a character in the **MCU**. Vellani is also a writer. She co-wrote comic books about her character. Iman Vellani has many talents!

DID YOU KNOW?
Iman [EE-mahn] is an Arabic word that means "faith."

Iman Vellani is best known for playing Ms. Marvel.

Vellani was born in Karachi, Pakistan, in 2002.

Growing Up

Vellani was born in Pakistan. When she was one year old, her family moved to Canada. The young girl loved to read. Her favorite character was Kamala Khan in Marvel Comics.

DID YOU KNOW?
Vellani loves the movie *Iron Man* (2008). She knows many lines by heart.

Surprising News

Vellani liked theater. But she did not plan to be an actress. Then her aunt told her that Marvel was looking for someone to play Kamala Khan, also known as Ms. Marvel. In 2020, Vellani sent **producers** a video about herself. They loved it and gave her the part!

DID YOU KNOW?
Vellani dressed up as Ms. Marvel for Halloween when she was 15.

Getting the role of Kamala Khan was a dream come true for Vellani.

Vellani attended an event for *Ms. Marvel* in 2022.

Ms. Marvel

Ms. Marvel came out on Disney+ in 2022. People loved Vellani's acting. She did a great job playing a teen girl with superpowers. Fans were excited to see more of Kamala Khan.

The Big Screen

In 2023, Vellani brought Khan to the big screen. She was in the movie *The Marvels*. Being in a movie with other superheroes was a lot of fun! Vellani was excited to work with actors she looked up to.

Vellani costarred in *The Marvels* with Brie Larson (middle) and Teyonah Parris (left).

Vellani inspires others to be true to themselves.

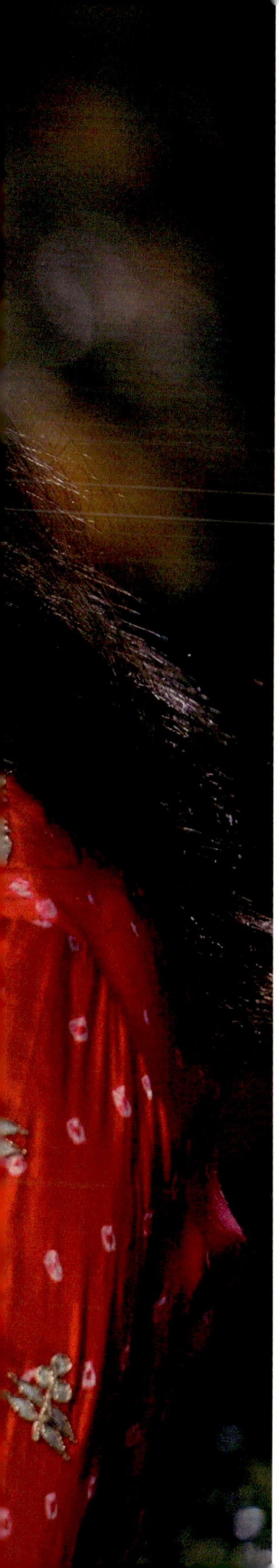

Something in Common

Vellani and her character had something in common. Both are **Muslim**. Vellani was happy to find a superhero who followed the same **religion** she did. Kamala Khan was the first Muslim superhero in Marvel comics.

Award Winner

In 2022, Vellani won a Saturn award for her work in *Ms. Marvel.* Fans and **critics** loved her performance. In 2023, she received the New Gold Award. It honored her as a leader in the Asian Pacific community.

In 2023, Vellani won the first New Gold Award for inspiring others with her acting.

Vellani helped write a comic book series called *Ms. Marvel: The New Mutant* in 2023.

Vellani the Writer

Vellani is more than just an actor. In 2023, she co-wrote four comic books starring Ms. Marvel. In 2024, Vellani wrote four more books in the series. These stories show Kamala Khan facing new dangers.

The Future

Vellani was not done with Marvel. In 2025, she played Khan's voice in an **animated** series on Disney+. It was called *Marvel Zombies*. As a young actor and writer, Vellani has a bright future.

From comic books to movies, Vellani is making her mark as an actor and a writer.

SUPER STATS

IMAN VELLANI

Birthday: August 12, 2002

Birthplace: Karachi, Sindh, Pakistan

Hometown: Ontario, Canada

Major TV Roles: *Ms. Marvel* (2022), *Marvel Zombies* (voice, 2025)

Major Film Roles: *The Marvels* (2023), *Animal Farm* (voice, 2025)

AWARDS

Saturn Award for Best Performance by a Younger Actor in a Streaming Series: 2022

Jury Prize for Best TV Actress: 2022

Vision Award for Best Performance in a Comedy: 2023

Critics' Choice Super Award for Best Actress in a Superhero Movie: 2024

GLOSSARY

animated A movie or TV show made with cartoon drawings.

MCU Short for Marvel Cinematic Universe, a shared universe of superhero movies and shows based on characters from Marvel comics.

Muslim A person who follows the religion of Islam.

producer A person or company who finances a movie or TV show.

religion The belief in and worship of a supernatural power.

READ MORE

Bray, Adam, and Knox, Kelly. **Marvel Studios Character Encyclopedia.** DK Publishing, 2024.

Kawa, Katie. **Iman Vellani: Making a Difference as a Young Superhero.** KidHaven Publishing, 2025.

ON THE WEB

IMDb: Iman Vellani
https://www.imdb.com/name/nm11940123/?ref_=nmtrv_ov

Kiddle: Iman Vellani
https://kids.kiddle.co/Iman_Vellani

Every effort has been made to ensure that these websites are appropriate for children. However, because of the nature of the Internet, it is impossible to guarantee that these sites will remain active indefinitely or that their contents will not be altered.

INDEX

About the Author

Joanne Mattern is the author of hundreds of nonfiction books for children. Her favorite subjects are biographies, sports, animals, and history. Joanne loves learning new things and sharing that knowledge with young readers! She lives in New York State with her family.